Painting a Thousand Words: Poems for Love to Return Home

Copyright © 2019 by Karibu Publishing

All rights reserved.

ISBN: 978-0-9971699-6-6
Electronic: 978-0-9971699-7-3

Edited by Wing Publishing. Layout and design by Phyllis Pollema-Cahill and Rosenna Bakari.

No part of this book may be reproduced in any form or by any electronic or mechanical means, including information storage and retrieval systems, without written permission from the author, except for the use of brief quotations in a book review.

Book cover artwork by Betz Smisek

For more information visit LawrenceDryhurstGallery.com

PAINTING A THOUSAND WORDS

Poems for Love to Return Home

**ROSENNA BAKARI
BETZ SMISEK**

Karibu Publishing

Rosenna and Betz dedicate this book
to people who are searching for that
special meaning in life.

May they one day come to understand
they are the special meaning of life.

PREFACE

Betz and Rosenna met through mutual friends. Although they had instant respect for one another, their personal relationship evolved much later after Betz attended a poetry reading by Rosenna. Rosenna reciprocated by visiting the Lawrence Dryhurst Gallery, where Betz's work is displayed exclusively. A conversation about how poetry and painting both touch the depth of the soul led them to ask more of each other.

Betz and Rosenna collaborated to have a poetry reading at the gallery to feed the souls of community members looking for a deeper human connection. Betz and Rosenna ultimately agreed that creating a relationship of collaboration would be the most inspiring, and they wanted something longer lasting than one event. Their desire to demonstrate love and compassion through collaboration culminated in this book *Painting a Thousand Words*.

Betz, a closet poet, not only agreed to perform with Rosenna, but they agreed to publish this book of poems as well. The purpose was to ignite the spark of love that people often forget, the love that has no opposite. Love gained is an opportunity to see our reflections in the world. Lost love brings the opportunity for growth and renewal. Love is neither selfish nor narrow. It spreads and flows like rivers, traveling long distances to sustain life.

Each poem is a tribute to the lessons of love. In a world where hope can seem lost for so many, these poems soothe the soul.

ABOUT THE AUTHORS

Rosenna Bakari

Rosenna is a seasoned writer. This is her fifth book. However, this book, Painting a Thousand Words, marks a new chapter in her enthusiasm for writing. She is co-authoring for the first time. This is also her first published book of poetry in spite of her 200 poem collection. In addition to writing books, she is a regular contributor to https://medium.com/@rosennab.

She earned her undergraduate degree in Psychology from Cornell University and her graduate degree in Counseling from SUNY Brockport. She earned her Ph.D. in Psychology from the University of Northern Colorado alongside her husband. They graduated together in 2000 while homeschooling their two children.

Other books by Dr. Rosenna Bakari

Too Much Love Is Not Enough (2018)

Tree Leaves (2016)

Original Sin (2016)

Self-Love (1995)

Betz Smisek

Imagination and creativity took root as a child and Betz has expressed herself through theater, photography, painting, stained glass and writing most of her life. As a published author of twenty-six children's books commissioned by the Chocolate Mountaineers of America, she looked forward to co-authoring this book of poetry with her selected works. Her inspiration comes from family, travel, and life.

When she is not writing, Betz is painting. She is currently the 'Artist in Residence' at the Lawrence Dryhurst Gallery in Colorado Springs, Colorado. Her paintings have been shown in galleries from New York to California. Her works are owned by major collectors in the United States as well as the Royal Family in Dubai.

Betz has her degree in Psychology and is a fourth generation native of Colorado Springs and lives with her husband Wayne in Colorado. She also is blessed with two daughters and four grandsons who live budding lives in Colorado and Idaho.

Other books by Betz Smisek can be found at Chocolatemountaineersclub.com.

CONTENTS

A MOTHER'S ADVICE 12
A SAMURAI CAME TO MIND 14
AN ARTIST'S CONCERN 15
AN UNGRATEFUL BODY 16
BECAUSE OF YOU 17
CLICHÉ 18
DANCING WITH THE DEVIL 21
DEFINING 26
DISHWASHER UNDER THE SINK 27
FOR MY DAUGHTER 31
GRACE 32
GROWING APART 35
GROWN-UP 36
HIGHER GROUND 40
HOW DOES THIS ARTIST CREATE 44
IN THE BEGINNING 46
KEY OF G 48
LOVE AT HEART 51
META-PHYSICS 52
MISSING YOU TONIGHT 53
MONSTERS 54
MOUNTAIN TOP 55

MY ADVICE ON CREATING	57
MY DAUGHTER, MY FRIEND	58
MY KITE	61
MY SOUL IS NOT READY TO DIE	62
OLD FRIEND	65
POSSIBILITY	68
RESOLUTION	71
RIGHT NOW	72
SEASONED	73
SHAKE IT OFF	74
STRANGE DAY	77
THIS ARTIST'S INNER CRITIC	79
THOSE CYCLES OF LIFE	81
THESE THREE WORDS	82
TRANSFORMATION OF A SUPER HERO	85
TRAVELING ADVICE	88
WHAT I WANT TO BE	89
WHAT WOULD YOU SAY	90
WHERE I COME FROM	92
WILL I STILL BE YOUR MOTHER?	93
YOU ARE	95
CONTRIBUTORS	96

A Mother's Advice

Fragments, fragments floating round
    Puzzle pieces lost then found.
    Multidimensional 3-D chess
    Will I ever get a rest?

New life coming—old ones dying
    Life circling once again.
    Kindness flowing—there's a knowing
    Is this all a test?

Rocks and symbols reassure
    That life is not just a blur.
    Life is more than downloaded junk
    At the whim of some celestial punk.

It's got to be from thoughts provoked.
It's got to have more poignant spokes!

Wheels need to be strong and tempered
    When moving from star to star.
    There needs to be strength and endurance,
    Coming from so far.

So many Paths to the ONE
Many hard and suffering and not so fun.

Then, there are the paths that zig and zag.
    They are the ones that won't let you lag.
    The ones that keep the interest up,
    The ones that constantly interrupt.

Those are not the paths for the weak at heart.
    The ones that want a walk in the park.
    Those are the paths for the adventurous type.
    The ones that need a jolt in life.

When things get dirty and out of place,
    And worries tip the balance of one's space,
    Venus' sunrise takes on a different hue.
    A soaring eagle is gone from view.

So, call in those squirrelly thoughts.
    Wash your face and say, "why not,"
    For an assumption can play a role.
    Then your actions can take a toll.

So runaway the makeshift day,
    Rhyme until it goes away.

Tripping, dancing out the door
    Stop—Enough—
    Say no more!

A Samurai Came to Mind

A Samurai came to mind wielding his mighty swords.
    His grace was dancing, but he was advancing,
    Reaching towards my cords.

I watch the forward movement, finding its way to me.
    I feared his swords would strike my world and sever all I see.
    It would change the way I look at things—change the very me!

It would rearrange my old wives' tales,
    Slash and shred those tattered sails,
    Separating me from who I'd been and
    Who I was thought to be.

Standing brave, I took a stance—
    Holding the threads I had sewn.
    Feeling them separate from my web,
    Divorcing all I'd known.

And as the Samurai walked away,
    A sign of accomplishment in his sway,
    I couldn't help absorb his tone,
    Feeling it strengthening my very backbone.

Regaining my balance, I stood up tall—
    I pushed away from my Wailing Wall.
    Breathing in my new fresh air,
    I set out on my new path focused and aware.

An Artist's Concern

If and when the power shifts while I am blending colors,
    Will the shapes pick their sides as if they've forgotten others?

Will all the darks get darker and shadow out the vision portrayed?
    Will all the lights lose their purpose and start to fade away?

Let's not forget the original desire of just wanting to relate.
    Imagine all will come together—no! It's not too late.

So Create!

For all the time it takes to paint is really timeless seeing.
    All the choices this artist makes only brings her into being.

An Ungrateful Body

So, what am I doing to make you so mad?
    Why are you making me feel so bad?

I've cut out white flour, sugar and salt—
    Taking antioxidants—it's not my fault.

I've eliminated partially hydrogenated oils—
    Only eating vegetables from decontaminated soils.

So, what's the big problem?
    Why are you so mad? Why do I have to feel so bad?

I've become non-alcoholic, decaffeinated and vegetarian,
    Peacefully meditating to flute music in my own solarium.

I've been exfoliated, colon-ated, realigned and re-lensed,
    Acupunctured, acid peeled, personally trained and cleansed.

I've been psychoanalyzed, hypnotized, decoded and transformed,
    Numeral-ized, astrona-mized, religu-lized and reborn.

So, what is your problem? Why the symptoms of distress?
    I've only been following the advice from the best!

Because of You

It is with gentle ease my creativity soars,
Rising high with every thought.
It quietly floats through heaven's doors
Where angels in prayer are sought.

Where forgiveness, kindness, and love abide,
And dancing notes in music ride,
It is there that,
Inspiration does not hide.

So, let the imagination go!

An artist is but a worried messenger always asking,
"Is it any good?"

"Was the message weak or lacking?"
"Did it say all it should?"

Rest assured that creation said its piece
For it came from deep within.

By letting go and finding that release,
Originality will always win.

Cliché

Life is too complex to live by simplistic clichés
Like, before you cross, look both ways
Maybe what you need is better peripheral vision
Maybe what you need is a bigger mission

Because clichés make for insensitive advice
You disconnect when words are too concise
Don't dismiss pain by saying it makes you stronger
Cuz pain ain't never made anyone's life longer
People in pain make desperate decisions
Cuz pain severely narrows its victim's vision

And no one finds comfort in the saying "they're in a better place"
When what they mourn about is never seeing their loved one's face
Amidst their pain life picks up the pace
You think you're comforting them
But that ain't the case

And don't ask me how I'm doing if you don't have time for conversation
Expecting the cliché, "I'm blessed" , without hesitation
If you're just glad to be alive
Then it's no wonder why you let that pain fester inside

And why in hell would anyone fight fire with fire
All that does is make the flames higher

"Winning isn't everything… spare a loser these words
Tell me something that I haven't already heard
Say something of value rather than words of convenience
Search your heart and make sure that you mean it
It's not about being original, just think before you speak
Designer phrases make a sentiment weak

Some say dog is man's best friend
Think again
Man is dog's best friend
Nobody follows a man around to pick up his shit
And you can teach an old dog new tricks

Most men actually prefer the kitty cat
But everything ain't beautiful just because it's black
Being black-balled will make you hang your head in shame
A black cloud means it's gonna pour down rain
So don't get overly attached to black
Sometimes it's just a warning to turn your ass back
And everything white damn sure ain't right
Remember when they said "don't follow the light"

Time is not money, money buys you time
A broke man always has worry on his mind
If your Facebook status is your most important update
Then your life status is pretty low rate
What you don't know can hurt you… ignorance is not bliss
Only a fool falls in love after the first kiss
There's no love at first sight that will make you blind
Don't spend your life waiting for that one of a kind
Nobody is really all that unique
We advance in life according to what we seek

The early bird doesn't always catch the worm
Sometimes the longer you wait, the more you learn
But life's not all about going too fast or too slow
Sometimes it's about knowing when to stop and when to go

You shouldn't have to fake it 'til you make it
Maybe you need to stir it up and shake it
Twist the words around in your head
Cuz clichés were created by people who are already dead
You too are dead if you can't be heard
So simplify life, but don't diminish words
If you find your own voice to bring words alive
Then you will be remembered long after you die

Dancing with the Devil

There is nothing to rely on
Nowhere to hide
All of you is exposed
Everything is outside
Your heart is on your shoulders
Your feelings are on your sleeve
You thought you were standing up
But you were crawling on your knees

Down on all fours
Looking at the floor

Boxed in by corners and walls
Wondering how you made that fall

Your over-stuffed pillows
Aren't keeping you up at night
It's your over-stuffed mind
Always ready to fight

Maybe it's a dream
Maybe it's lucid
Even in your sleep
Life shouldn't get this stupid

Nah, you're fully conscious
This is all real
The devil's eating you up
Like you're his last meal

Here's some advice
To keep you from getting devoured
Clean up your life
Take a long hot shower
Shower your consciousness
Empty your mind
The calmness you seek
Doesn't come from wine

A Course in Miracles says
"Nothing real can be threatened"
The safety you seek
Can't be secured with a weapon

Hope and faith focus on the unknown
But the present moment
Is where grace is shown
Say yes to the universe
Embrace your pain
Live in truth
Lies are worse than shame

You need nothing to rely on
You don't need to hide
Live life exposed
Everything on the outside
Open your heart
Accept the feelings on your sleeve
You'll find courage to stand up
If you pray on your knees

Step by step you'll cross the floor
With a new vision that moves you
Toward the door

Now there are windows
Where there used to be walls
You're too well-grounded
To even worry about a fall

A worry-free mind is a cozy pillow at night
Now that you seek peace
Instead of looking for a fight

It's not a dream
It's your life that's lucid
Don't sleep through it
Or it will get stupid

Stay fully conscious
This is all real
Make the devil spit you out
And find a new meal
You're now at the head of the dinner table
Commitment to humanity
Keeps your own life stable

Use your words wisely
Make sure you encourage
All those around you will also flourish
Because you, they rely on
So they don't have to hide
When they feel too exposed
You take them inside

Your open heart
Accepts the feelings on their sleeve
You give them courage to stand up
When they are crawling on their knees

Light up the world
Fix something that's wrong
Live your life like the 23rd Psalm
Walk through
The valley of the shadow of death
Fear no evil as long as you still have breath
You need nothing to rely on
Nowhere to hide
Everything you need
You have
Inside

Defining

Will I always meld into others
Like fluid acrylic paint?
Flowing into another's composition
Despite my own personal fate?

Will I always melt like hard butter
Left out in the sun too long?
Feeling the pain in your eyes first and
Forgetting my own song?

Why can't I be an old oak tree solid and rooted deep?
Why do I stand tall at first until my branches start to weep?

What makes my boundaries readjust as if I am conquered territory?
Why do I feel disheartened, not remembering my own story?

It isn't that I mean to flow out of the lines so free.
It's just that I lose my way and can't see the forest for the trees.
I can't focus on just one thing.
I would tear off my clothes if I couldn't sing.
I can't be made to sit still for long.
Oh, what would it be like to not feel so wrong?

SO
Don't stop my dance.
Don't trip my feet and end my run.
Listen harder to the music.
My music—that is still being sung.

Dishwasher Under the Sink

A favorite story I love to share
Is about a mother who raised a daughter with great care
Privileged in the suburbs where she felt safe at night
She never even learned how to fight

Mom spent a bunch on extra-curricular activities
Trips around the world and extravagant festivities
She raised her like a princess destined to succeed
She gave her anything she thought she would need

But there was this experience that made mom think twice
She wondered if she was loving at too high of a price
When one summer she left her princess
With relatives in the hood
When asked to wash dishes
Little princess replied
Of course she would

But for 5 minutes she just stood around
She looked from side to side
She looked up and down
'Til her auntie came in and asked

"Sugar what you looking for?
Why is the dish rag on the floor?"

*"I dropped that cloth while I
was checking all the drawers,
But I never found what I was looking for.
You asked me to wash dishes
But I don't see a machine.
How do you expect me to get the dishes clean?"*

Auntie lifted up Princess' manicured hands
Gave her rubber gloves and told her to use the dish pan
Perplexed and confused, Princess did wash the dishes
But with her hand in the water she made three wishes
One—since there was no dish washer
That they would use paper plates
Two—if she were old enough to wash dishes by hand
She was old enough to date

The last wish was that she wouldn't visit again soon
Her idea of a vacation was not washing forks and spoons
There was also no central air, so Princess was hot
And she definitely didn't like sleeping on a cot

Princess didn't wait to get back to her suburban home
She interrupted her parents' vacation
And called them on the phone

When mom heard the frivolous
Complaints coming from her daughter
She gave the phone to her husband
Because her eyes started to water

Princess missed the lesson in community
She was being taught
Would she ever understand?
Family comfort can't be bought
When you're with family you love
Circumstances don't matter
But snubbing your nose up at relatives
Nothing could be sadder

So when Princess returned home, mom removed the tiara
She traded in her BMW for a Cutlass Sierra
She didn't take away all the gadgets of comfort
But she took away enough
For Princess to realize
Happiness doesn't come from having a lot of stuff

Now Princess knows that power and privilege
Are just that
No one should ever use it
To turn their back

On those less fortunate
With little material gain
Who at least don't worry
About going insane
From trying to protect
Their precious status
Despite wealth
The privileged seem to be the maddest

At age 12
This was a lot for Princess to understand
But she pondered it
Along with memories
Of sleeping under the fan
Since that summer Princess
Changed the way she thinks
But she never stopped cherishing
The dishwasher under the sink

For My Daughter

With kite tails may you soar
    Dancing on star cluster trails,
    Knocking on victory's door.

At wisdom's hearth may you keep the fire,
    Manifesting your dreams,
    Striving for all you desire.

In angel's wings may you rest
    Having slain all your dragons
    Becoming your very best.

For you are your own reality
    Creating
    Whatever you care to be.

But regardless,
    Live your life abundantly
    And always remember to be free.

Grace

He spends his day chasing tomorrow

The only way he knows how to deal with his sorrow

After living with pain for so long

When things go right

They still feel wrong

He struggles to pay debt

He doesn't even owe

Contentment in his life is stop and go

He walks around

With a smile on his face

While pleading for God

To show him Grace

But the pain keepa comin'

Like the train on a track

Seems ain't no way to turn it back

If Grace ain't showed up

In half a century

                He figures

It's something just ain't meant to be

Get right back up every time he falls down

But the blues follow him around

What in Heaven, what in Hell

In the fifteenth round

Will he be saved by the bell?
He hopes in the end
He will win by decision
And all his sins will go into remission

While sleeping at night with demons in his head
Angels hover blessedly over his bed

She lay beside him wrapped in his arms
Wondering how he could be so strong
Her pain has her depressed and insecure
He professes his love
But she still feels unsure
Skeletons in her closet
Keep her fears alive
Loving him is the way she survives
Innocence stripped away at an early age
Forty years later
She still can't turn the page
At least he helps her cover the book
He tells her to close her eyes
And just don't look
But the boogie man still stares her
In her face
As she pleads to God to show her Grace

And the pain keepa comin' like the train on a track
Seems ain't no way to turn it back
If Grace ain't showed up in fifty years
            She figures
She'll spend the rest of her life
Hiding tears
In his arms she can hide forever
His love makes her life a little mo' betta
Between them
They have 100 years of pain
Beneath all the hurt love still remains

They gaze in each other's eyes
To feel at ease
The touch of their lips
Is a warm summer breeze
He turns her tears into joy
And she turns his blues into the sky
Their tenderness is purified
The pain will keepa comin'
Like the train on a track
But their love is big enough
To hold it back

Growing Apart

Forever leaving—pushing pulling
Will she ever go?

Album pictures—sweet remembrances
Oh God, I'll miss her so.

Wringing hands and furrowed brows
The panic of 'What ifs.'

It's time for you. It's time for me.
Please desolation lift!

For you are you and I am me
And we are not the same.

It's good you go. Take care—be brave.
It's life you need to tame.

She called last night, and all was right.
We talked of boyfriends, school and life.

We laughed finding our needs were less.
But I still felt the pangs of emptiness.

For nothing could ever fill that space.
No one will ever take her place.

Grown-up

When I was just a little lad
Being young seemed so sad
I dreamed of the day when someone would call me "Miss"
Every birthday that was my wish
I couldn't even wait to be a teen
Though Momma warned being grown
Ain't what it seems

When I finally aged enough
To put away the toys
I had to learn to make smart choices
About the little boys
Balancing books, boys and sports
Was quite an act
And some social skills I realized I lacked
Momma reminded me that
All the world is a stage
And I couldn't go back
To the toy-playing age
I must respond to the curtain call
And be ready to play my part
In a blink of an eye the stage lit up
The show was about to start

Bill payer, renter, employee
Were all my roles
Childhood was snatched right out
From under my nose
Being on your own is not the same
As being your own boss
Years would be spent building my own
Bridges to cross
Pay myself first, save for a home
Having a man is OK
But so is being alone
Live and let live, bury the past
Remember people are more important
Than cash
Don't expect a standing ovation
Always work out of a
Sense of dedication

So many lessons and advice
That I couldn't keep up
I kept falling down like a new born pup
Momma said when I fall
Just fall to my knees
The Lord would pick me up
And have me swinging in the breeze
Every now and again she tells me

"I tried to tell you so
But when you were 15
You thought you knew all you needed to know"

She still held my hand in hard times
And assured me that soon my own path I would find

Just when I got steady on my feet, along came marriage with kids
A family of four squeezed up for story time in a king-size bed
But that didn't last long because soon the children started to get the itch
Passing down your hardest lessons to your children is the parenting glitch
As they defy you and tell you how they can't wait 'til they are grown
They can't wait to be away from you in spite of all the love you've shown
And you tell them about life being a stage
But everything you say they interpret as old-age

Generation after generation, the cycle will continue
And only grown-ups know what is on the adult menu
Now that I'm all grown up there are days I long to sit on Momma's lap
Especially when I feel like someone forgot to give me the road map
Day after day I push and I pull

My cup doesn't run over, but it sure is full
There are days I don't know where I'm going or how to get there
When childhood feels like the dream and being grown-up
is the nightmare

Higher Ground

Keep your head up girl,
There's something God wants you to have,
You think that life's
Been taken away from you,
But there's something
God wants you to grab.

You've been a servant for many years.
He knows your joy, He knows your fears.
God's making room for something big in your life.
But in order to see it you can't focus on your strife.
Right now a path is simply being cleared
To make room for you to move around.
He doesn't want you
To move backwards
He wants you to move to higher ground.

It's easy to get caught
Like a deer in headlights
When those we love depart.
Life crashes into us at high speed
And that's where our troubles start.
You slip into an emotional coma.
People all around reach out to you
But you can respond to no one.

Wake up girl and realize
All you have are flesh wounds.
Nurse it with faith and acceptance
And your heart will heal real soon.

The doctor you serve
Is on call twenty-four hours and seven.
He wants you to have peace on earth
Not wait 'til you get to heaven.
God's not trying to punish you,
So don't spend time pondering sin.
God's always bringing you joy
Making sure that you win.

So think big, expect more,
Look for abundance girl,
Don't focus on your loss
Christ died for you 2000 years ago
To show you how to carry a cross.
Knowing that your spirit is bigger
Than any circumstance at your door.
Sometimes we have to let go of things we love
For God to bless us with more.
More wisdom, more wealth, more passion, more purpose
More of everything good
God has gone before you just like the Word said He would.

So don't wait on God, He's already passed by
And left a care package on your step.
In it there's a note to remind you—
Even Jesus wept.
But let each tear that rolls down your face
Lead you to your purpose.
When you can hear the burning bush whisper in your ear
You'll know your pain was worth it.

You now stand on higher ground
And you can not be moved.
No matter how rocky the path may look
Each step you take is smooth.
Your head is cool, your heart is calm
Your presence is collected.
Self-pity, grief, discouragement
Are useless – so they're all rejected.

Though your heart was broken and torn,
It's no longer sad and lonely.
You wear a genuine smile again,
Your life is a true testimony.

On higher ground you can see that joy is present
In spite of your past.
You inhale faith and exhale peace,
And thank God you are free at last.

How Does This Artist Create

I fall through the lens of God's eye—
Fall deep within.
Oblivious to the surrounding sounds.
Isn't that what God intends?

What do I see looking out?
I'm making something out of nothing.
Maybe that is the way it starts—
The void of nothing's something.

Black as black—still looking back.
Do I know which way to go?
In denying my sense of self,
Will I lose my soul?

My Creations don't just start
As if they know what to do.
They don't just move along with well intentions,
Always knowing who's who.

I have to trust that some shape will form
And fill its void of space.
Not having a specific color palette
Won't be my saving grace.

Working fast I have come to know,
Creates what wants to be seen.
Having no time for obsessing ego,
I tend to produce a work more pristine.

SO
Creating from nothingness
Takes courage then, surrendering from within.
And by staying in the mind's eye of God
Just may keep my paintings from the dustbin.

In The Beginning

In the beginning there was a void.
The void had an inkling—
And it was good.

The Observer Observed and became aware.
The relationship began.
Being aware of the awareness, it created light.

And the light started the darkness into motion.
The darkness converted into Energy—swirling and dancing.
This too, was good.

Energy changed and exchanged, causing vibration.
It vibrated so fast a new form from its lightning was born
—sound.
The faster it moved the more it spun sound—electrifying,
threading music into creation.

Then suddenly—
Energy took shape.
The shape grew and expanded, no longer contained, no
longer sheathed.
Explosion—the birth of existence—the known.

And so, it continued to grow.
More expression.
More layers.
More form.
More color.
More dimensions—
ART!

Creation started to slow for it was tired.
Spinning changed to whirling.
Whirling moved into a wobble.
It fell over and rolled around until it stopped.
It looked back on its creation and smiled.

"I am that, I am."

Key of G

It happened in the key of G
with circumstances not suited for me.
The melody was fine at first until I was told
I had played it in reverse.

And so, I thought if I turned it around
and played the tune upside down,
the notes would unscramble, and all would be clear—
I really didn't need to hyperventilate out of fear.

Time dragged on and the notes moved to F
and all of me was barely left,
But I realized I finally understood the key of G,
and all the rest was now okay with me.

Then, all the songs moved into symphonies—
They were combining all the notes, including the key of G.
Still confused with the A's and B's,
the C's and D's were again a mystery to me.

But I knew a few notes, so I had no fear.
I just needed to pay attention and persevere.
I would never give up and turn back around,
Not with my music bordering on the profound!

I tried to convince the teachers how creative I could be.
Surely, they'd see the genius in me.
Yet it was not surprising when they chose to be done,
shaking their heads, their hands all rung.

So, I went to the park and talked to the falling leaves.
I needed to figure it out, so, I rolled up my sleeves.
It's not just knowing the notes within me, myself, and I.
There has got to be more pieces to this pie.

But, to throw out the baby and keep the bathwater
may lose that innocent sound.
Yet, how do I know if the notes are coming together
if I'm the only one around?

So again, I went seeking not hiding—
determined to keep my boat from capsizing.
I went back to the music room at the top of the stairs,
trying not to notice unkind kids and their unkind glares.

Their music sounded off and the volume was loud.
Yet they appeared not to notice and acted very proud.
Well, I didn't show up for the tryouts after all—
The last chair was filled anyway, and she was already
heaving notes against the wall.

So, I ended up going back to the park
only bringing my harmonica as old as Noah's Ark.
Children were dancing to their own sounds of invention.
Just listening to their music made me blow my harp with intention.

I played and I played, and I played some more—
Children came running as if they knew the score.
They joined in and melded with my A, B, and C.
Suddenly, there was that familiar Key of G.

This time I understood and had an opened heart.
Children tend to help one see a larger part.
Playing in reverse doesn't really matter all that much.
Or should playing upside-down make one feel so out of touch.

It's all in the freedom of expressing,
the laughter and fun.
Music tends to harmonize and come together
when it's not just one-on-one.

Love at Heart

Why do you feel so familiar when I hardly know you at all
I feel like we've made love a hundred times
Yet I'm afraid to make love to you
Even once
My hands long to touch you
But they don't know how
My heart knows I love you
But my mouth can't speak the words
You've stolen a piece of my heart
That will never belong to anyone else
Seems the only reason I sleep at all
Is for a chance to dream of you
Lying in your arms soothes me
Like a hot bubble bath
With my favorite music playing
Are you one more thing that's wrong
In my life
Or are you the only thing that's right
I won't beg for you to stay
If you say you have to go
I won't take you for granted
As long as you are here

Meta-Physics

Nothing is more real than the existence of our nonexistent Love

I can't touch it, but I can feel it

I can't see it, but its beauty infatuates me

I can't hear it, but I follow the sound of its whisper

I taste it on the tip of my soul

And I smell its sweet aroma fill the air all around me

Our love is not physical, but metaphysical

It existed long before we manifested time and space

Our love is expressed without motion but mystified with Emotion

Stronger than the waves of the midnight ocean

Our love is not even psycho-logically sound
        But the sound of its logic can be found
            In the cycle of the universe
                …Predictable

Like the moon phases and the solar eclipse

Like the rotation of the earth around the sun

It turns winter into spring…

Missing You Tonight

Where are you?

Another no-show tonight?

Nowhere to be found on the evenings I fight

The demons in my head that tie my stomach in a knot

I'm the one that the sandman forgot.

Eight hours, eight minutes, eight seconds

Just a wink,

I'll take whatever time

I can get not to think.

One little pill

Should be my ticket to dreamland.

Six hours later,

I'm still starring at the fan.

What I wouldn't give tonight for a snore

Before morning comes and my feet touch the floor.

I shut my eyes and try to meditate,

The deep breathing I can appreciate,

'Til my mind wanders

Between my future and past,

Relaxation simply doesn't last.

Sleep avoids me like a neglected child,

While all the thoughts run through my mind like wild.

Sleep don't come easy is what they say

I know it all too well, as I watch night turn to day.

Monsters

Have you ever been alone in the night,
When somehow a monster just comes into sight?

It appears in the corner or under your bed
It's all you can do to pull the covers up over your head.

"Whew!" you say. "I'm safe for now and out of sight.
Oh, if only I could get to the light!"

"Is it a Fah-wa or a wall-wart? I can't rightly see.
Oh, if only someone would come and rescue me.

But the next thing you know there's light in your room
And in that corner was just your stuffed baboon.

And the noise you had heard under your bed,
Well, it was just a silly ole thought you made up in your head.

Mountain Top

There are days I have such clarity
Einstein's genius doesn't even compare to me
I live the moment with no resistance
Let it all unfold without persistence
Que Sera, Sera,
What will be, will be
No such thing as a missed opportunity

The love that was lost is better off dead
The words that were forgotten are better left unsaid

Life feels like one big WOW
Over forty years, but I feel like a child
I laugh with the universe
Because I have no tears to cry
I'm not even interested in the rhetorical "why"
Self-pity teases me to come out and play
But I stand firm, today's not the day
I have a vision and x-ray eyes
I see right through my own lies
I'm at the mountain top looking down
My head is fit to wear a crown
I hear the burning bush whisper in my ear

"In this place there is no fear"
I feel personal power erupt within
I start hoping tomorrow I'll feel it again

Then I catch myself and return to the now
I take a deep breath without making a sound
I know life for me isn't always this clear
So I try to hold the moment dear

The phone rings, I check caller-ID
Voicemail takes it and my mind remains free
My conversations have to be positive
This is the moment I choose to live
I'm not delusional or grandiose
I've simply chosen a path with more gratitude than most
It's not well traveled, no tracks to lead the way
In order to stay on it I have to pray
Not to an angry God waiting to punish
My soul's connected to the only "One Is"
When the day is over and I lay down to sleep
I'll ask the "One Is" for my soul to keep
As my head hits my pillow and I reflect on my day
I see that the universe's glory was on full display

My Advice on Creating

Do not waste this day by crying over yesterday.
Write!
Grab hold and think a thought. Just start!

Breathe in deep and blowout slowly. The paper will ignite.
Be Ready!
Be Bold!

Have more words on hand in case a thought takes hold.
For God's sake,
Keep going!

Don't stop and judge the ashes that fall.
Unless the fire goes out and that's all.
Don't quit!
Start again!

Don't leave when your eyes burn and your back begins to hurt.
When your fingers are cramping,
And your mind has gone berserk.

Open books and tear out their pages.
Crumple up those words and use them for kindling.
Remember the stages?

Suddenly your creation takes hold and you feel the flame grow.
Stay with it!
Feed it with desire. Now it's starting to show.

Your creation has taken off and is creating itself.
Be happy!
Be grateful!

A possible bestseller is heading for the shelf.

My Daughter, My Friend

I can still hear myself saying in my head
Don't try to be her friend
Just be her mother instead
Guide her with loving discipline
Protect her from the world
Do whatever necessary
To take care of baby girl

I nursed you on my breast
Carried you on my hip
Read book after book
For the best parenting tip
You taught yourself how to walk, talk and read
While I was busy figuring out how to take care of your needs

I noticed that you stayed close beside me and watched my every move
So I tried to make life look easy and smooth
Even when life's trials caused me to shed some tears
I tried not to pass along to you my fears
But you looked in my eyes and saw my pain
And your maturity sheltered me like an umbrella in the rain
You cried with me, gave me hugs and told me I was going to be alright

Now baby girl was nursing mommy who couldn't sleep through the night
When I told you the color finally came back in my life so I could smile
You said "Momma, color never left, you just became color blind for a while"
In that moment I knew you'd become my friend
A woman to woman relationship with you had begun
So I want to be the friend that you always admire
But still be my daughter that I need to inspire
I want to give you confidence to stand on your own
And still know that I will never leave you alone
I want to show you how to follow and teach you how to lead
As well as when to fight and when to concede
I'll always remind you that a boyfriend is only an accessory
Make no one in your life or nothing a necessity
You came into the world with only the spirit of God
On that alone must you ultimately rely
Be real with yourself and don't pretend
Always listen to the spirit within
You are who you are
From I am who I am

Don't spend your life trying to please me or them
You have already shown me who you are
I'm watching and waiting for you to go far
Yesterday you were a guinea pig learning to speak

Today your voice is strong, no hint of being weak
You are tomorrow's butterfly spreading her wings
Ready to take on whatever life brings
Joy is what you bring to my life each day
And there is this sentiment I am trying to convey
You were born my daughter as a godsend
But the biggest blessing is that now you are my friend

My Kite

If I had known the kite would sail so high,
I might never have picked up the string.
I might never have launched into the sky.
I might never have loved the dear thing.

It tugs at my hands—wanting more—wanting more.
Afraid to hold tight, I let it soar—let it soar.

Oh, what if I lose the dear thing!

It climbs higher and higher
Growing smaller and smaller.
I wind quickly to bring it back in.

It drops and plunges—dips and lunges.
I let go and it's up again.

Oh, if I had known the kite would sail so high,

I might never have picked up the string.
I might never have launched it into the sky.
I might never have loved the damn thing!

My Soul Is Not Ready To Die

I'm more than alive, I am living
How do I know, because my heart's still giving
There's beauty everywhere I take time to notice
My laughter does not depend on how funny the joke is
My mouth falls open and my lips curl
With an acceptance of my insignificance in the world

Remain attentive—Pay close attention
To all the significance that don't get mentioned
I pay attention to the parts that make the whole
I invite emptiness into my soul
Take out the garbage that clutters my brain
So peace is all that remains

I know I'm living because
I'm growing like a flower
Stretching out to embrace
The universe's power
Following cycles and changing seasons
Recognizing my purpose
Without looking for a reason

If I drift off to sleep I'll fall from Heaven
So I stay alert—twenty-four, seven
Nothing in the world is what I seek

I'm so still I feel my heart beat
Its rhythm reminds me to stay in tune
Distractions come too easy and too soon
I recognize the danger of living amongst the dead
And remain cautious not to let ghosts in my head
I avoid addressing ghouls from an ego identity
That obstructs my serenity

Dead folk run around the earth everyday of their life
With bad intentions or emotional strife
Buried alive under ashes of resistance
While seeking happiness that's beyond subsistence
Creating more pain in themselves and others
No understanding about how to keep brothers

Even I've gotten a taste of hell's fire
It's where broken souls retire
Full of wrinkles from unforgiveness
And premature aging as a result
Of bitterness
Once I felt the singe on my surface
I realized clinging to negativity
Ain't worth it
So I spread my wings
Headed toward the sky
Because my soul was not ready to die

Now I'm living, born again
With nothing to lose and even less to win
The only time I acknowledge is now
I hear the voices that don't make a sound
Because I listen without the need to talk
Instead of running through life, I take my time and walk

I know I'm living when I run long miles,
Write poetry, perform, or grant warm smiles
Expressions of my harmony with The One
That makes the tulip open
only for the sun

Old Friend

I woke up one morning and didn't find you there
Seemed like you just disappeared, but I didn't know where
I knew I should just let you go, but couldn't resist temptation to look for you
As I thought about all of the crazy things that you sometimes made me do
I searched in my journal, but all I found were words
Pain—you were gone
Instead of being happy, I thought something had to be wrong

You'd been by my side for quite a while
Did you get tired of hiding behind my smile
I tried my best not to give you any play
But didn't think you'd ever go away

I never did like the company you keep—Pity and Grief
They've taken me through more changes than a fall leaf
I have to admit, though, you brought me closer to God
Prayer is what kept my spirit alive

With you not here I feel so free
I like how life now looks to me
The rain has stopped, the sun is shining
I won't waste no more precious time whining
My tears are dry, my eyes are clear
Blue Jays singing is what I hear

I've learned all from you, Pain, that I need to know
I'm now moving to a place where you can not go
My spirit has invited me to move to higher ground
I can't have you there trying to bring me back down
You didn't leave empty-handed—I had baggage for you to take
It was time for me to start over with a fresh, clean plate

When I tried to leave before something pulled me back
But this time I knew I was on the right track
There's plenty of other fish in the sea for you
But I gotta do what I gotta do

Now that you're gone, I'm changing the lock
I won't open the door, so please don't knock
My head and my heart have been renovated
I'm in a new space—you can't invade it
You'll have to find yourself a new home
Don't even try to call, I won't answer the phone

Besides, you wouldn't even recognize me anymore
Since I've picked up some presents from the "here and now" store
I live only one moment, one day at a time
The past and future no longer pre-occupy my mind
Besides, I know that's where you like to hang out
Looking for companions to share guilt, shame, and doubt
I hope it will be a long time before our paths cross again
I'd rather just remember you as—well—"an old friend"

Possibility

Possibilities are endless, not limited to A, B, C, or D

Open your mind and your heart, and choose to be free

There is no happiness formula

Life calls your name

And you form to her

The path is not linear

It is full of circles and curves

Walk it barefoot

If you dare have the nerves

To not let people confine you to a box

Climb through the window

If a door is locked

When you are free

Remember from whence you came

Victory is not a dance because

Life is not a game

So if you point the gun

Be prepared to shoot

Because infinity is infinity

But it is not absolute

It usually ends with

Different versions of the truth

So don't get played trying to play the field.
Instead of trying to control others
Master your own will
Ahhhh—the paradox of mastering your
Will without becoming your own slave
The world is so much bigger
Than your small-mind-cave
You can't buy freedom
You have to choose it
When you don't make a choice
Then your choice is to lose it
No looking for magic
Hoping for a grade
You are the only star
Of the New Year's Parade

The world is watching with no interest at all
So where you end up is your call
Don't let pain stop you
It is only your guide
That forces you to pause
Just to take a look inside
It's not there to paralyze
Or put you in a coma
So keep your head up
And follow the aroma

Until you smell sweet success inviting you close
But you have to make the choice that scares you the most

Odd, different, weird
You they will describe
because the world is not at all round in
Your eyes
You can choose to come out of your shell
Or stay in your cocoon
You can crawl on the ground or
Will yourself to the moon
Because the sky is not the limit
When you live life like you're in it
It's not a video game
A spectator show
You get to change the rules
To get where you want to go

Possibilities are endless, not limited to
A, B, C, or D

But the choices that you make
Will determine if you are free

Resolution

My heart lets go and pours magic potion over my face.
I feel my spirits lifting. I'm dancing in space.

But there were times when I filled my mind with agonizing perceptions.
Retelling and reliving my stories with elevated misconceptions.

I'd conjure and feed the heaviest deceivings—
Not wanting to let go of the feel of survival achievings.

Well, I'd earned those legendary badges, having sewn them on my sash.
After all, they represented the triumphs of my survival.
No way was I going to throw them in the trash.

But their representation was of destructive intent—
Keeping alive twisted interpretations of a mind so bent.

And the unhappiness never seemed to wash away,
Nor my feelings of regret for those who had betrayed.

So, deciding to discard that cherished collection was quite invigorating,
Reducing the sash to ash proved to be rather liberating.

Because change does not happen when hording one's sash of sorrow,
Opening old wounds of memories kept alive into the morrow.

No! A sash should be a banner saying, "It was hell! But, I'm okay."
And no longer living in the past as if it were today.

Right Now

I am caught between two worlds waiting to be born.
I am neither here nor there.
My definition has changed, and the new language has not yet been written.

Oh, Women of the new beginning hear my cry.
Do not turn back to the toil even though the warmth of the hearth is inviting.
If nothing else, stand still where you are until the warmth of the sun reaches you.

I wait for the glimmer of the first sign of light.
I wait knowing the pink in the sky is the start of good to come.
I wait frozen from the night but not dying—only cold.

My fate is in my hands, which are in the hands of God.
But only he can thaw this Goddess Neophyte—this beginner of knowings—
This female who reddened the earth with her blood of creation.

She cries for justice against the betrayal of the old world.
She no longer will march to the drum of other women's beatings.
She wants understanding and appreciation for her sacrifices.

Oh, Women of the new beginning
Do not turn back to the toil of what no longer fills your womb with joy.
Stay aware and rethink.
If nothing else, stand still until you see the promise of pink.

Seasoned

I don't mind howling winds or blinding snows,
Nor violent rains before any rainbows.

I don't fear building storms with distant flashes,
Darkening skies with their noisy cloud clashes.

Because I can deal with any weather
No matter what it is wearing.

I can see it coming and know the color,
No matter what it is preparing.

I am a seasoned sailor— a voyager of the seas.
I am the strongest survivor—the knower of the breeze.

I will wear longer than the lady at the bow.
I will fare better after the oceans mighty row.

For the seas will eventually settle down
With their waves receding to an easy flow.

And the weather will always change its mind,
For experience has taught me so.

Shake It Off

I don't want to write another love poem about you
The love we had proved to be untrue
I ain't gonna write you
Another love poem
What happened between us
Was all wrong

So why, as I sit down by the still pond
Do ripples of love for you
Run through my mind
Not a single breeze against my skin
Yet shadows of love
Are blowing in the wind

Ignore the stanzas coming into my head
Run around the pond instead
Cook, clean, sew — do anything
To resist what my heart
Is trying to bring

Been down this road
It was a dead end
Now I'm supposed to believe
That love is just around the bend
Maybe, but what about
The dead curve just ahead
I don't have anymore tears to shed
I refuse to pick up the pen, I refuse to write
But I toss and turn all through the night

When I saw you yesterday
I should have kept my distance
Hearing you call my name
Broke through all my resistance
I never should have touched your arm
I became possessed by all of your charm
Why did I ever let our eyes meet
Now it's you that my soul seeks

Now the only way to deal
With these feelings are verse by verse
If I don't pick up the paper
My heart will be cursed
But once I write, love becomes real
And love for you I don't want to feel

Maybe some Tylenol pm
Will help me sleep it off
When I wake my heart won't feel so soft
Two pills later and counting sheep
I feel myself fall off to sleep
Finally no more thoughts about this man
But when I woke in the morning…
… This poem was on my night stand

Strange Day

One day the moon
Contradicted the sun
The tides disobeyed
The gravity of the moon,
Salmon coasted downstream
And Earth's axle
Shifted a hair of a degree

On this day I looked into your eyes
And fell in love with you
As mysteriously and strangely
As all the other occurrences
That went unnoticed by everyone
Who busied their lives with living –
Including you.

Still, you must have felt something
Because you stopped by my life for just a minute
You sat a spell,
Long enough for me to fall deeper in love
With your hugs, kisses and smiles

But you never made
yourself quite comfortable
It's like you kept your shoes on
And stayed close to the door

Eventually, a loud roar came
From the sky
And as mysteriously
As I fell in love with you,
I fell out of love with you,
As you walked out the door –
Without closure

This Artist's Inner Critic

An Angst has cast its powerhouse beat
Causing an underground bruise.
I'm told that it is part of the balance,
When winners have to lose.

It seems to realign the dancing lights,
When they are out to play,
Shadowing all the good portrayals
Sending confidence away.

It lowers the light of the evening sky
Without a moon to see.
It closes all the open doors
Stopping the air that I breathe.

Oh, Angst be gone and stand aside!
Must we always fight?
Must you always wet blanket life,
Blading the string of my kite?

I know your name! You are concealed in fear.
Your mask hides your seductive persuading.
I command you go! Get out! It's clear.
Your voice is truly fading.

For I can throw masses of color
Over those weakened hues.
I can change the very subject matter,
Portraying other views.

So, move aside, dear Angst.
Don't waste your energy on me.
Your voice no longer has a hold.
I paint footloose, for I am free.

Those Cycles of Life

It is the passing through
   The sluffing off,
   The giving over,
   And the letting go.

It is in the surrender
   That slows the heart,
   Calms the fear,
   And deepens the breath.

It is the waking up
   That creates the awareness,
   Moves the darkness
   And brings the Dawn.

It is the looking, focusing, then seeing
   That puts it all in motion.
   The moving, pushing, bearing down,
   That brings new life.

And so
It is another skin shed
   The leaving behind.
   An arduous escape out
   And into the nakedness of the beginning.

The start of another ring of the tree
   The end the start, the last the first,
   The beginning of another circle out and back
   And so it continues— In the passing through

   Those magnificent cycles of life.

These Three Words

He'd said he loved her a thousand times
But not one instance
Came to her mind
Three simple words
She wanted to hear
Never fell upon her waiting ear
More and more impatient she grew
She kissed his mouth
To draw the words out
But the continual silence
Made her heart doubt

He'd said he loved her a thousand times
But not one instance came to her mind
She'd utter to him each night
Before falling to sleep
His lack of reciprocation
Started to make her weep
Did he want the relationship to grow
Or was he trying to let her go?
In his eyes she noticed a gleam
But didn't know if he was as happy
As he seemed

He'd said he loved her a thousand times
But not one instance came to her mind
So out of frustration she decided to part
Since she thought she could never
Capture his heart

Once he was gone she missed him so much
How he always smiled
His gentle touch
He treated her like a lady
Opened every door
Whatever she asked for
He offered her more
He took pictures of her
Hung them all around
And he loved taking her out
For a night on the town
He introduced her to his family
As his queen
And not one word out of his mouth
Was ever mean
But she only heard the words
That he did not say
The words that he used
His actions to convey

Because she didn't know love's language

Her heart experienced

Unnecessary anguish

He'd said he loved her a thousand times

Since he left, every instance comes back to her mind

Transformation of a Super Hero

Behind your mask you hide pain, hurt, and scars
Hidden from those close to you
As well as those looking from afar
You disguise yourself as a super hero
Never allow anyone to see you soar low
The days when you are too weak to fly
You turn your back, determined not to cry
Thinking, what kind of super hero
Would you be
If you couldn't protect
What kind of image would you project

Yes, the world expects you to be strong
Even your best friend
Doesn't know when something's wrong
But don't blame your loved ones
For what they've never been told
Because you've invested so much
Into your super hero role

You are never the problem
You're the problem solver
Problems you don't fix today
You promise to fix tomorrow

Sometimes you dig a hole so deep
You make promises
You shouldn't even try to keep

People call on you when they need a hand
Playing into your image of the ideal Super man
After a while you can't tell if people like You for you
Or if they simply like
All of the helping you do

Those who really love you are just as confused
And worried about you just getting used
But you dismiss their concerns
Underneath your cape
Cause saving the world is your escape
But after you save the world your own sorrows remain
You see that there is nothing personal to gain

Who will explain to the super hero
That the net gain is always zero
When you hide behind a cape and mask
Your true identity no one will even ask
But the day you show yourself
To the world
Will be like opening
An oyster and finding a pearl

Your warm smile is beautiful
But so are warm tears
Being brave is mighty
But so is admitting your fears
Every hero needs boundless strength
But rest for the weary is also meant
Super heroes don't have to be perfect
Being human is sometimes worth it

Traveling Advice

The distance catches sight of itself—
It sees far and near.
It caters to its length and breadth.
But plugs its mighty ears.

For hearing tends to bend its path,
Sending it left and right,
Changing all the markers,
Losing familiar sights.

To hold its end is quite a trick,
For chaos whips within—
But strength withstands and calm returns,
As Ego fails to win.

What I Want To Be

I don't want to be the kind of light
That draws moths and mosquitoes to
Soap bubbles in a dish of water on a table.

I don't need to be a lighthouse
That searches all night for stranded and weary sailors,
Trying to find their way back home.

There are plenty of bright bulbs and tall beacons already
in the world.

I want to be the flame of a candle
That gently flickers and brightens a moment of darkness,
Helping others find a way back to their own path, again.

What Would You Say

What would you say if I allow you to speak
Would you explain that your flesh was too weak
Would you deny that you knew
My feelings would be hurt
Would you continue apologizing
For treating me like dirt

What would you say if I decided to listen
Would you try to convince me
Our love you been missing

Would you try to win back my heart
Would you beg for a brand new start
Did you really think because we didn't have sex
That our relationship could end without regret

My feelings for you were
Love at first sight
So I had to resist making love to you
With all my might
'Til you invested in the relationship
With a willingness to fall
Instead we're both paying the penalty
For your early withdrawal

There's no point in me making myself listen
My ears don't need to hear
What my heart's already missing

Where I Come From

I come from a gene pool of a family revived,
Of dreams realized,
And destinies for future generations capitalized.

I come from the earth school of lessons reinstated,
Ideas incubated,
And true self-awareness emancipated.

I come from a knowing of silver spoons,
Joys and sorrow,
And a Universe full of guarantees for tomorrow.

Will I Still Be Your Mother?

Will I still be your mother,
    When all the sands have gone out to sea,
    When all the bark has left the tree,
    And I am just a memory?

Will I still be your mother,

When trusted realities turn into happenstances,
    And all my horses have lost their prances,
    When years of striving have fogged my senses,
    No longer strong enough to mend my own fences?

My dreams will grow fainter from aging decisions,
    With the memories lingering, clouding visions.
    And is that bell tolling no longer clear?
    Or is that just another one of those mother fears—

YES! I will still be your mother.

For each mother mothers in her own unique style,
    Only getting to rub and polish those rough edges for a while.
    For yours too, will be gone as fast as you left,
    Bumbling and tripping out of your nest.

And someday you'll ask your own perfect human being,
  "Will I still be your mother now that you're doing your own thing?"

And hopefully yours will assure you to read between the lines,
  For mothers are anchored in sacred eternity for all times.

You Are

You are the river that leads me astray
To designs of magical landscapes at play,
To scenarios full of a kaleidoscope's colors,
Mingling and dancing with all of the others.

You are the stream that polishes my creation
In patterns of sifting and shifting sensation,
In rolling tumblers of ancient stones
Washing away—no longer alone.

You are the pond that settles my commotion
Of models of an old tired emotion,
Of stirring sediments from worn out grooves
Gentling perceptions—calming my moves.

You are the ocean that feeds my desire
With plans of wonderment set on fire,
With sparkling and bubbling of future scenes
Igniting the spirits to all that it seems.

Contributors

Poems by the Authors

Rosenna Bakari

CLICHÉ.	18
DANCING WITH THE DEVIL	21
DISHWASHER UNDER THE SINK	27
GRACE	32
GROWN-UP	36
HIGHER GROUND	40
LOVE AT HEART	51
META-PHYSICS	52
MISSING YOU TONIGHT	53
MOUNTAIN TOP	55
MY DAUGHTER, MY FRIEND	58
MY SOUL IS NOT READY TO DIE	62
OLD FRIEND	65
POSSIBILITY	68
SHAKE IT OFF	74
STRANGE DAY	77
THESE THREE WORDS	82
TRANSFORMATION OF A SUPER HERO	85
WHAT WOULD YOU SAY	90

Betz Smisek

A MOTHER'S ADVICE	12
A SAMURAI CAME TO MIND	14
AN ARTIST'S CONCERN	15
AN UNGRATEFUL BODY	16
BECAUSE OF YOU	17
DEFINING	26
FOR MY DAUGHTER	31
GROWING APART	35
HOW DOES THIS ARTIST CREATE	44
IN THE BEGINNING	46
KEY OF G	48
MONSTERS	54
MY ADVICE ON CREATING	57
MY KITE	61
RESOLUTION	71
RIGHT NOW	72
SEASONED	73
THIS ARTIST'S INNER CRITIC	79
THOSE CYCLES OF LIFE	81
TRAVELING ADVICE	88
WHAT I WANT TO BE	89
WHERE I COME FROM	92
WILL I STILL BE YOUR MOTHER?	93
YOU ARE	95

www.ingramcontent.com/pod-product-compliance
Lightning Source LLC
Chambersburg PA
CBHW020947090426
42736CB00010B/1308